THE LOCAL FOOD PROJECT

Lisa Fingleton

GW00779217

One day I bought a BLT sandwich in a petrol station and I couldn't believe that there were over 40 listed ingredients from all over the world, including such things as Diglycerides of Fatty Acids, xanthan gum, emulsifier and stabilisers.

BACON, LETTUCE & TOMATO

Cooked smoked back bacon with tomato, lettuce & mayonnaise on malted wheat bread.

INGREDIENTS: Malted Wheat Bread [Wheat Flour (**Wheat** Flour, Calcium Carbonate, Iron, Niacin, Thiamin), Water, Wholemeal **Wheat** Flour, Malted **Wheat**, **Wheat** Gluten, Yeast, Salt, Malted **Barley** Flour, **Soya** Flour, Emulsifier (Mono- and Diacetyl Tartaric Acid Esters of Mono- and Diglycerides of Fatty Acids), Dextrose, Preservative (Calcium Propionate), Palm Fat, Rapeseed Oil, Flour Treatment Agent (Ascorbic Acid)], Cooked Smoked Back Bacon (22%) [Pork Back, Salt, Smoked Water, Antioxidant (Sodium Ascorbate), Preservative (Sodium Nitrite)], Tomato (15%), Lettuce (11%), Mayonnaise [Rapeseed Oil, Water, Pasteurised **Egg**, Spirit Vinegar, Pasteurised **Egg** Yolk, Sugar, Salt, Dextrose, Stabilisers (Guar Gum, Xanthan Gum), Concentrated Lemon Juice, Flavouring (contains **Mustard**), Paprika Extract].

ALLERGY ADVICE: For allergens, including cereals containing gluten, see ingredients in **bold**.

CAUTION: Although every care has been taken to remove bones some may remain.

STORAGE: Keep refrigerated. Not suitable for home freezing. Use by: see front of pack. Once opened, consume immediately.

No artificial flavours or colours.

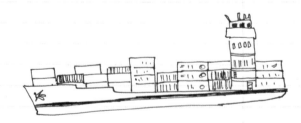

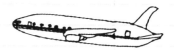

I started to think about the journey of a sandwich and where all these ingredients come from. It felt like this sandwich connected me to so many places, people, plants and animals from all over the planet. I started to think about the energy needed to bring this sandwich to me; all the electricity, fuel and water. It makes me sad that food, which lands on our plate, has travelled thousands of miles just to be eaten by us.

I had been to Borneo and seen the destruction of the rainforest with palm oil plantations and here was palm oil in my sandwich.

THINK OF YOUR
FAVOURITE SANDWICH....

How far does your sandwich travel before it reaches you?

How many ingredients make up your average sandwich?

How much of your sandwich is made up of 'real food' and how much of it is manufactured ingredients, made to taste like 'real food'?

How many planes, boats and trucks are involved?

How many women, men and children are involved in picking vegetables and minding animals around the world?

What conditions do the animals live in?

Where does your food come from?

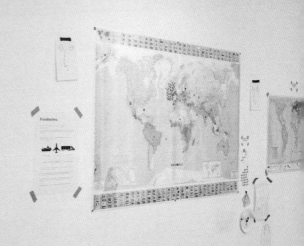

Foodmiles

The Sandwich Project. Installation Shots from VISUAL Carlow, 2018
Co-curated with Stephen Alwyn
Image: Ros Kavanagh

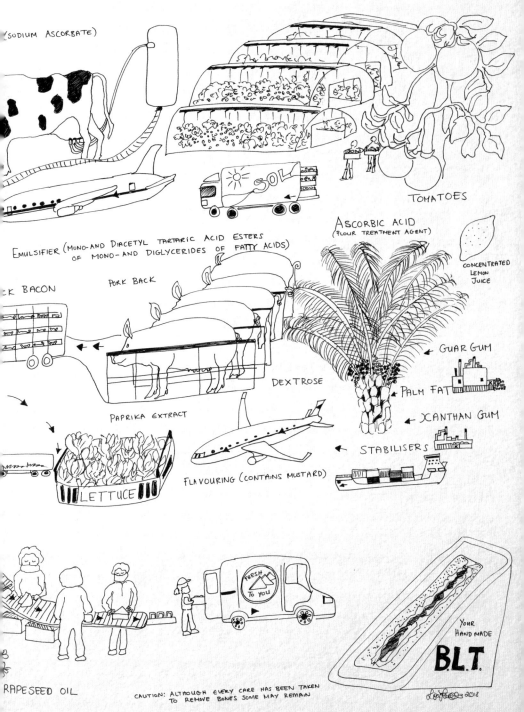

(SODIUM ASCORBATE)

TOMATOES

ASCORBIC ACID
(FLOUR TREATMENT AGENT)

CONCENTRATED LEMON JUICE

EMULSIFIER (MONO- AND DIACETYL TARTARIC ACID ESTERS OF MONO- AND DIGLYCERIDES OF FATTY ACIDS)

K BACON

PORK BACK

GUAR GUM

PALM FAT

DEXTROSE

XANTHAN GUM

PAPRIKA EXTRACT

STABILISERS

LETTUCE

FLAVOURING (CONTAINS MUSTARD)

FRESH TO YOU

YOUR HAND MADE B.L.T.

RAPESEED OIL

CAUTION: ALTHOUGH EVERY CARE HAS BEEN TAKEN TO REMOVE BONES SOME MAY REMAIN

2018

I learned a lot from that BLT sandwich.
It reminded me that there is no such thing as 'cheap' food.

Someone, somewhere is paying the price in terms of poor conditions for workers, crowded conditions for battery hens or health implications for the consumers of processed foods. Long haul food tends to be pumped with preservatives and wrapped in plastic so that it appears 'fresh' after travelling half way round the world.

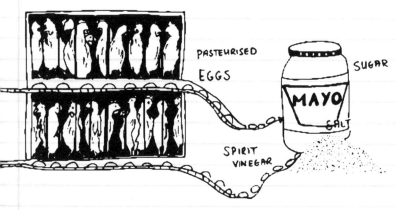

The Sandwich Project, Installation Shot from VISUAL Carlow, 2018
Co-curated with Stephen Alwyn
Image: Ros Kavanagh

Lisa Fingleton

"Only 1% of Irish farms grow vegetables, the lowest in the EU"

Agriland headline based on Eurostats Report, October 2016

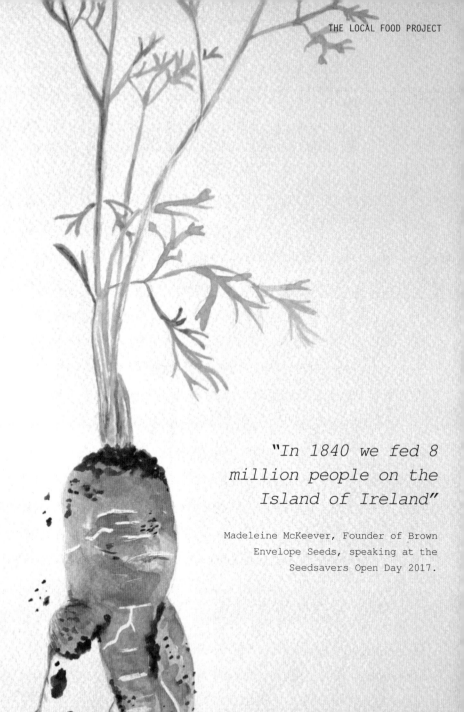

"In 1840 we fed 8 million people on the Island of Ireland"

Madeleine McKeever, Founder of Brown Envelope Seeds, speaking at the Seedsavers Open Day 2017.

Why are we not growing vegetables in Ireland?

It feels to me that Ireland, as a country, is less independent and resilient than we were when our state was founded. We import most of our food even though we can easily grow everything we need. I believe we need to reclaim our independence and resist globalisation and systems of capitalism which value monoculture and short term profit over diversity and sustainable agriculture.

We live on an island and have a unique opportunity to become a world leader in organic food production. We have the rain and the soil!

Yet today in Ireland, farmers are subject to the whim of international quotas, trade agreements and supermarket chains, which flood the market with vegetables at below cost price.

We closed our sugar factories and now import millions worth of sugar a year. Indeed 'Siucra' is now the property of a German company called Nordsucker and Hughes Brothers (HB) Ice Cream is subsumed into Unilever.

DUE TO ADVERSE
WEATHER
CONIDTIONS THE
MUSGRAVE TRUCK
WAS UNABLE TO
DELIVER ANY STOCK
TODAY.
APOLOGIES FOR ANY
INCONVENIENCE
CAUSED.

With ever-changing weather patterns, transport is becoming more disrupted. Even after a few days of snow, the shops started running out of food.

We are privileged in that we grow most of our own food. My partner, Rena, and I have a garden and polytunnel. We know how delicious fresh vegetables taste when they are picked straight before mealtime.

Food that is picked too early can never be as tasty as food that is left to ripen in the sun. Supermarket produce just doesn't have the same taste as it is picked weeks before it is ripe and stored in cold storage before being transported half way around the world.

It amazes me how marketing campaigns convince people that this food source is more desirable than what is available fresh and seasonally in the field next door.

I WANTED TO DO SOMETHING
PRACTICAL. I DECIDED TO START
BY EATING ONLY LOCAL FOOD.

I was really inspired by Barbara Kingsolver's book 'Animal, Vegetable, Miracle', in which she wrote about her family's year of eating locally in America. I wondered if I could do the same in Ireland?

It is not easy to eat only Irish food for a year and I know that. There are hungry months in late spring when the food is just not ready after late frosts.

So I decided to do a 30 day local food challenge. September seemed a really good option as the garden is truly abundant with tomatoes, kale, spinach, herbs, peas, beans, onions, garlic, beets, carrots, parsnips and the list goes on. It is a luscious month in the gardening calendar.

BY EATING ONLY IRISH FOOD I HOPED TO:

(1) reduce food miles and carbon footprint

(2) reduce single use plastic.

(3) support local growers and farmers.

(4) eat food that is tasty and fresh.

(5) resist capitalist systems that insist that food is only about profit

(6) engage in a conversation with the community around me, about what we are eating and how we can be more sustainable in our food consumption

(7) raise awareness about climate change

To eat Irish still means doing without what Barbara Kingsolver called the 'botanically outrageous' foods that we import, but it is somehow easier in September with all the food on offer in the garden and hedgerows.

GUIDELINES FOR THE
30 DAY FOOD CHALLENGE

I decided that the challenge would only include
food so I could drink what I wanted.

I would eat only food that was 100% grown
and produced on the island of Ireland. All the
ingredients would be Irish with a 5% margin in
the event of extreme hunger.

If someone offered me food, on the basis that is was
Irish, I would accept it.

I also decided to share what happened each day
online and invited other people to take part.

I wrote lists of the haves and have-nots…Could I really live without chocolate, pasta, rice, ginger, oranges, pepper, spices, avocados and every other imported delight to which I have become so accustomed?

WHAT'S OUT?	
BANANAS	☐
ORANGES	☐
CHOCOLATE	☐
SUGAR	☐
ALL IMPORTED FOOD	✳
RICE	☐
PASTA	☐
LENTILS	☐
NUTS	☐
GINGER	☐
SPICES	☐
AVOCADO	☐

WHAT DO WE GROW?	
	☐
SPUDS	☐
CARROTS	☐
ONIONS	☐
GARLIC	☐
KALE	☐
CABBAGE	☐
TOMATOES	☐
LEEKS	☐
CHILLIS	☐
APPLES	☐
RASBERRIES	☐
BLACKCURRANTS	☐
HERBS (OREGANO, BASIL THYME, MINT)	☐
	☐
	☐

As with most challenges I avoided it until the last minute and found myself waking up on the first of September with no forward planning and more importantly no shopping done. Thankfully, for breakfast we had some Irish porridge and milk and I munched on some peas on the way to my first meeting.

The REAL challenge was avoiding sugar! I didn't realise
I was so addicted to sugar until I tried to come off it.
That was a shock. I was used to having something sweet
to nibble on every time I had a cup of tea or coffee (and
I have lots of those).

A friend is a brilliant cook and she had the most
amazing spread of sweet things when I arrived to her
house for a meeting.

"I will resist, I will resist".

LIZ'S HONEY FLAPJACKS RECIPE

Gas Mark 4/180
Serves: 16

INGREDIENTS

300g porridge oats
200g butter
7 to 8 tablespoons honey

Line a baking tray
with parchment
paper.

Melt the butter over
a low heat. Stir in
the honey and mix
for a few minutes.
Now, add the oats
and stir well, so
the oats are evenly
coated. Spread the mixture evenly on the
baking tray and press down.

Pop in the oven for 15 to 20 minutes,
until the top is slightly golden.

Leave to cool completely, cut in to
squares and enjoy!

Thankfully a friend of mine Liz, came to
the rescue and made me a tray of honey and
oat flap jacks which helped to quell the sugar
cravings (even if I was still dreaming about
chocolate éclairs).

One of the best things about doing the 30 Day Local Food Challenge was making connections with passionate and interesting people. People started doing the challenge too and sharing their recipes and ideas.

I linked in with Transition groups and visited organic community gardens. I was met with such generosity of spirit. Willie dug up colleen potatoes in the lashing rain, smiling all the while, in his illuminous yellow jacket.

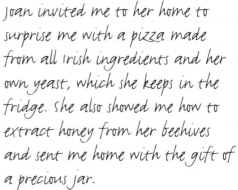

Joan invited me to her home to surprise me with a pizza made from all Irish ingredients and her own yeast, which she keeps in the fridge. She also showed me how to extract honey from her beehives and sent me home with the gift of a precious jar.

No Woman is an island

I had a lot of fun as friends and strangers around me started engaging in the challenge. One day Jean opened her door as I passed the house and invited me into her polytunnel to share her Ballybunion grapes.

Isabella and Evan bartered eggs for vegetables. I visited their yard for the first time and have never seen such happy hens, or such elaborate hen houses. The highlight was the pink and blue Barbie style palace, perched on the side of the hill overlooking the sea, complete with pink trays to collect the eggs.

The most challenging times were days on the road when I didn't properly prepare my food in advance. One night I drove from Waterford to Kerry after the annual 'Grow Fest' conference and I couldn't find anything to eat in 'convenience' shops along the way. All of the fruit was imported and even the quick cook porridge had sugar in it.

TAYTO
CHEESE + ONION
€1·00

KING CHEESE + ONION
€1·00

KP MINI CHIPS
€0·80

KP RANCHEROS
€0·90

TAYTO SALT + VINEGAR
€1·00

TAYTO HOT CHIPS
€1·00

It was definitely easier on the days I worked from home as we had a garden full of food.

Lisa Fingleton

"In these times when geography becomes virtual and developers urbanise the earth, may the farmer continue to hold true ground keeping the intimate knowing of the clay alive"

John O Donoghue 'For the Farmer'

During the 30-Day Local Food Challenge I realised that there is an increasing disparity between what we are eating and growing. There is a greater distance than ever between the farm and the fork. We need to take action if we want to be more self-sufficient and healthier!

I also learned that I couldn't eat most 'local' artisan food products as much of the raw ingredients are imported and it is only their 'added value' that brands them 'Irish'.

WHAT CAN WE DO?

Lisa Fingleton

GROW YOUR OWN!

Dig up your lawns and plant vegetables. The revolution starts in your front field or balcony!

Create community gardens and allotments. Link in with local Transition or GIY (Grow It Yourself) groups.

SUPPORT LOCAL GROWERS

If you don't have a lawn or are attached to the one you have you can buy from growers directly, shop at farmers markets or local organic food shops. You can also join CSA (Community Supported Agriculture) scheme. A CSA scheme means you get a regular box of vegetables and the grower gets a regular income.

If we want tasty, healthy, local food we need to directly support the people who grow it.

FORAGE

Remember there is so much free food in Ireland. Our ditches, fields and coastlines are full of abundant food supplies (though avoid areas that are sprayed with chemicals): Blackberries, wild mushrooms, elderflower, damsons, sloe, nettles, water cress, seaweed and the list goes on. Take part in foraging workshops so you can identify all the edible treats around you. Remember to share with nature!

LOAF

Remember to buy LOAF when you can:

LOCAL

ORGANIC

ANIMAL FRIENDLY

FAIRTRADE

Check labels carefully. 'Produced in Ireland' may mean that it is only packaged here.

SAVE SEEDS

Save your own seeds and link in with organisations like
'Irish Seedsavers' to help protect heritage plants.

CONSERVE WATER

Find ways to save water and adapt your garden to changing water patterns.

The so-called 'hosepipe ban' prohibits you from watering your vegetables with a hose, which in turn makes it extra difficult to grow vegetables. Be creative!

THE HOSEPIPE BANDIT

BEE THE CHANGE

Bees are in serious danger and we need to protect them, not just because, without them we have no food!

Become a beekeeper or if you can't do that, create a bee-friendly garden where bees have plenty of pollen and no harmful chemicals.

Buy local honey as it is great for your health to eat honey from your local biosphere.

The important thing is to start taking action. Do something simple today.

We can all BE the change we wish to see in the world

Lisa Fingleton

Artist Studio

Bee Drawing, Culture Night, Siamsa Tíre, 2016
Image: Aoife Fitzmaurice

ARTIST BIO

Lisa Fingleton is an artist whose practice incorporates drawings, collaborative projects, film, documentary and immersive installations. Much of her work is rooted in the autobiographical and deals with sociopolitical and environmental concerns. The artist lives and works on a small farm in North Kerry and has spent many years cultivating deep-rooted connections between art, food and farming.

Lisa is concerned about the fact that we are importing so much of our food and losing the capacity to be self-sufficient, despite what we know about climate change and carbon footprint. She strives to 'be the change' she wishes to see in the world and likes to walk the talk, grow the food and integrate life with her studio practice. For the last number of years she has been working closely with her partner Rena Blake. Together they are consciously focusing on the 'local', organising projects and events on the home farm such as community tree growing, foraging, 'meitheals' and other ways of engaging local people in global issues around food and sustainability.

www.lisafingleton.com

Photos: Lisa Fingleton, Rena Blake,
               Ros Kavanagh, Aoife Fitzmaurice

Drawings: Lisa Fingleton

Design: Pure Design

Printing: GPS Print

Publisher: The Barna Way

ISBN: 978-1-9993175-0-8

Acknowledgements:

This publication was created with the assistance of the Creative
Work Bursary Award from Kerry County Council Arts Office. Work
was created with the support of the Arts Council of Ireland,
Siamsa Tire and VISUAL Carlow. Thanks to Rena Blake, Padraig
Cunningham, Kate Kennelly, Catríona Fallon, Denise Reddy,
Michelle De Forge, Paul Hayes, Emma Lucy O'Brien, Steven
Alwyn, Niamh Ní Dhuill, Ian McGregor, Claire O'Connor, Thomas
O'Connor, Barbara Derbyshire, Dee Keogh, Transition Kerry and
EVERYONE who participated in the 30 day local food challenge. A
special thanks to my parents who gave me my passion for eating
local food.

Holding True Ground, Solo Exbition/Installation, Siamsa Tire, 2015